Mastering DIGITAL PHOTOGRAPHY

Isaiah A. Jackson

Copyright

Copyright © 2024 by Isaiah A.Jackson

Dedication

To all the moments that made me pick up the camera,

To the mentors and friends who fueled my passion,

And to every photographer who has ever doubted their

potential

This book is for you. Keep capturing the world as only you

see it.

TABLE OF CONTENTS

INTRODUCTION

THE HISTORY OF PHOTOGRAPHY

UNDERSTANDING CAMERA FUNDAMENTALS

MASTERING COMPOSITION AND LIGHTING

4 THE ART OF POST-PROCESSING

5 LIGHTING TRICKS

6 SPECIALIZED PHOTOGRAPHY SETUPS

7 PRACTICAL TIPS FOR ASPIRING PHOTOGRAPHERS

Welcome to the World of Photography!

Photography is not just about taking pictures; it's about capturing moments, telling stories, and preserving memories. In this book, we'll dive into the fascinating world of photography, starting from its origins and evolving into the diverse and powerful medium it is today.

INTRODUCTION

My Journey from Frustration to Fulfillment

It was a crisp autumn afternoon when I found myself standing in front of a breathtaking landscape, camera in hand, feeling utterly defeated. The scene before me was a perfect symphony of colors golden leaves gently swaying in the breeze, a river reflecting the vibrant sky, and the soft glow of the setting sun casting long shadows across the earth. Yet, as I reviewed the images on my camera's screen, they fell short of capturing the magic that unfolded before my eyes. The colors were flat, the details blurred, and the essence of the moment lost in translation.

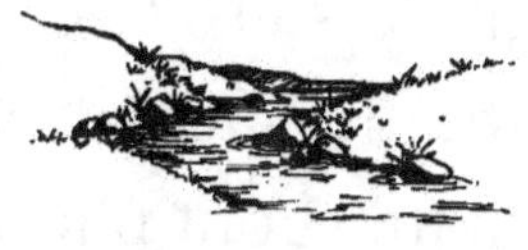

If you're reading this, chances are you've felt that same frustration. Perhaps you've taken a shot that didn't quite turn out as you'd hoped, or maybe you're just starting out and feeling overwhelmed by the sheer amount of information out there. Whatever your experience, I want you to know that you're not alone. Every photographer, no matter how skilled, has faced these challenges. But the good news is that with the right guidance, you can overcome them and that's exactly what this book is here to provide.

In the pages that follow, you'll find a practical, step-by-step guide to mastering photography. Starting with the basics, ensuring you have a solid understanding of your camera and its functions. You'll learn how to manipulate the Exposure Triangle (aperture, shutter speed, and ISO) to achieve the perfect balance of light and shadow. You'll also learn the composition techniques that will help you frame your shots in a way that tells a compelling story. As you advance, you'll discover how to tackle more complex scenarios, like capturing the subtle beauty of a nighttime cityscape or the dynamic energy of a long exposure.

But this book is more than just a technical manual, it's a companion on your creative journey. I'll share with you the lessons I've learned, the mistakes I've made, and the moments of triumph that have kept me passionate about photography.

You'll hear stories of real-world challenges I've faced, from shooting in unpredictable weather to working with difficult lighting conditions, and how I've used these experiences to grow as a photographer.

By the time you reach the final chapter, my hope is that you'll not only have a deeper understanding of photography but also a newfound confidence in your ability to capture the world around you in all its beauty. Whether you're looking to document your travels, create stunning portraits, or simply express your unique perspective, this book will equip you with the skills and knowledge to do so.

The world is full of moments waiting to be captured, and with the right tools and mindset, you'll be ready to seize them. Turn the page, and let's start transforming your passion for photography into a skill that will last a lifetime.

CHAPTER ONE

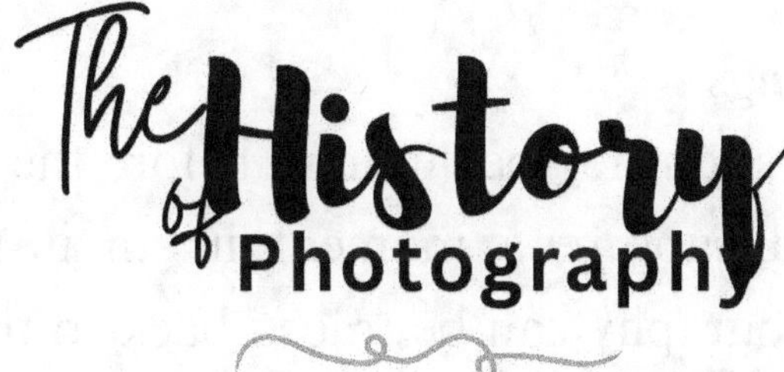

The History of Photography

Why is History Important in Photography?

A grasp of the history of photography is like unlocking the secrets of a time capsule. It allows us to see how far this art form has come, from the painstaking early days to the digital age we live in today. Knowing where photography started and how it evolved gives us a deeper appreciation for the craft. It also connects us to the pioneers who paved the way, turning what was once a laborious and expensive process into the instant, accessible medium we enjoy now.

A grasp of the history of photography is like unlocking the secrets of a time capsule. It allows us to see how far this art form has come, from the painstaking early days to the digital age we live in today. Knowing where photography started and how it evolved gives us a deeper appreciation for the craft. It also connects us to the pioneers who paved the way, turning what was once a laborious and expensive process into the instant, accessible medium we enjoy now.

Early Beginnings

Photography's journey began long before the click of a camera could capture a moment in an instant. The roots of photography can be traced back to the ancient use of the camera obscura "a simple device that projected an image of its surroundings onto a surface". This concept was known, but it wasn't until the early 19th century that the first photograph was created. In the 1820s, a French inventor named Joseph Nicéphore Niépce managed to capture a view from his window using a process called heliography. This early photograph, known as "View from the Window at Le Gras," took several hours to expose, resulting in a grainy but revolutionary image. It was far from the instant photos we take today, but it was a start "a monumental leap forward in the quest to preserve moments in time".

Development over Time

The 19th century was a period of rapid development for photography, marked by significant milestones that shaped the medium. In 1839, Louis Daguerre introduced the daguerreotype, a method that greatly improved the process Niépce had begun. Daguerreotypes were widely celebrated for their clarity and detail, but they weren't without their drawbacks. The process involved long exposure times, often requiring subjects to remain perfectly still for several minutes. Additionally, each daguerreotype was a one-of-a-kind piece, unable to be reproduced (a limitation that photographers would soon seek to overcome).

As the century progressed, so did the technology. In the late 1800s, George Eastman introduced the world to film photography, a groundbreaking advancement that would change the landscape of photography forever. Film allowed photographers to capture multiple images quickly and efficiently, no longer bound by the constraints of the daguerreotype. This innovation also laid the foundation for color photography, which began to take shape in the early 20th century, adding a new dimension to the art form.

The Digital Revolution: A New Era

The late 20th century brought the next major transformation in photography with the advent of digital cameras. In the 1970s, Kodak engineer Steven Sasson invented the first digital camera, a bulky device that recorded images onto a cassette tape. The images were rudimentary by today's standards—black-and-white and low resolution—but they represented the beginning of a seismic shift in how images would be captured and processed.

By the 1990s, digital cameras became more accessible and began to replace film cameras in both professional and consumer markets. The introduction of digital single-lens reflex (DSLR) cameras allowed photographers to have the same control over their images as with traditional film cameras but with the added benefit of instant review and the ability to edit images on a computer.

The 21st century has seen photography become an integral part of everyday life. Smartphones now come equipped with high-quality cameras that rival dedicated cameras from just a few years ago. Social media platforms like Instagram and Facebook have turned everyone into a photographer, with billions of images shared daily across the globe.

Think about the last time you took a photo, whether it was a selfie, a shot of your lunch, or a beautiful sunset. Chances are, you took that photo with your smartphone, edited it with a filter, and shared it online within minutes. This instant sharing of images is a far cry from the days of daguerreotypes and film, and it has transformed photography from a specialized craft into a universal form of communication.

Influential Photographers

Throughout history, certain photographers have left an indelible mark on the art form, shaping the way we see the world through a lens.

Ansel Adams is one such figure. Known for his stunning black-and-white landscapes of the American West, Adams mastered the interplay of light and shadow, creating images that are as much about emotion as they are about scenery. His work not only highlighted the beauty of the natural world but also raised awareness about the importance of conservation.

Another iconic photographer, **Dorothea Lange**, used her camera to document the human condition during one of America's most challenging periods "the Great Depression". Her iconic image, "Migrant Mother," is a haunting portrayal of a mother's struggle to survive during the Dust Bowl era. Lange's work with the Farm Security Administration (FSA) brought attention to the plight of displaced farmers and poor families, using photography as a tool for social change.

Henri Cartier-Bresson, often called the father of modern photojournalism, introduced the world to the concept of the "decisive moment." Cartier-Bresson believed that the most powerful images were those that captured a fleeting moment when the composition, lighting, and subject all aligned perfectly. His candid, unposed photographs of everyday life across the globe have become some of the most celebrated images in photography history.

CHAPTER TWO

Understanding Camera Fundamentals

Photography is a blend of art and technology, where your creative vision meets the mechanical and digital tools that bring it to life. At the heart of this process is the camera, the tool that captures the world as you see it. Understanding the different types of cameras and how they operate is crucial for any photographer, whether you're a beginner just starting out or an experienced professional looking to refine your skills. In this chapter, we'll explore the three primary types of cameras used today: DSLRs, mirrorless cameras, and smartphones.

Camera Types: DSLR, Mirrorless, and Smartphones

DSLR Cameras (Digital Single-Lens Reflex)

Digital Single-Lens Reflex (DSLR) cameras have long been a favorite among photographers due to their robust features, reliability, and the exceptional quality of images they produce. From beginners to seasoned professionals, DSLRs cater to a wide range of photography needs.

How they work:

The core component that sets DSLRs apart is their mirror mechanism. When you look through the viewfinder of a DSLR, you're actually seeing the scene through the camera's lens. Here's how the process works:

1. **Light Entry:** Light enters the camera through the lens.

2. **Mirror Reflection:** Inside the camera body, a mirror sits at a 45-degree angle, reflecting the light upwards.

3. **Viewfinder Display:** The reflected light travels through a pentaprism (or pentamirror in more budget-friendly models) and out through the optical viewfinder, allowing you to see the scene in real-time.

4. **Shutter Release:** When you press the shutter button, the mirror flips up, momentarily blocking the viewfinder.

5-   **Image Capture:** The light then passes directly onto the image sensor, capturing the photograph almost instantaneously.

This rapid mirror movement is one reason why DSLRs are excellent for capturing fast-moving subjects like sports or wildlife.

Key Features:

DSLRs are packed with features that make them versatile tools for a variety of photography styles:

Interchangeable Lenses:

DSLRs allow you to swap out lenses, making them adaptable for different photography situations. Whether you need a wide-angle lens for sweeping landscapes, a macro lens for close-up detail, or a telephoto lens for distant subjects, DSLRs have you covered.

1

Manual Controls:

DSLRs provide full manual control over exposure settings like aperture, shutter speed, and ISO. This level of control is crucial for photographers who want to create images that match their exact vision.

2

Optical Viewfinder:

The optical viewfinder in a DSLR offers a real-time, clear view of the scene without any lag or delay, something that is highly valued by photographers who need precision in timing, such as in action or sports photography

3

4

Battery Life:

DSLRs generally have a longer battery life compared to other types of cameras, as the optical viewfinder does not require power like the electronic viewfinders in mirrorless cameras. This makes DSLRs especially suitable for long shoots.

Advantages:

The versatility of DSLRs makes them suitable for almost any type of photography. Whether you're capturing portraits, landscapes, sports, or wildlife, a DSLR can handle the task. The availability of a wide range of lenses allows you to experiment with different focal lengths and perspectives. Additionally, the robust build quality of many DSLRs means they can withstand tough conditions, making them reliable tools for photographers in any environment.

Examples of DSLR Cameras:

Canon EOS 5D Mark IV: A professional-grade camera with a full-frame sensor, ideal for high-quality photography and video recording

Nikon D850: Known for its exceptional image quality and resolution, it's a favorite among landscape and portrait photographers

Nikon D850: Known for its exceptional image quality and resolution, it's a favorite among landscape and portrait photographers

Canon EOS Rebel T7i: An entry-level DSLR that offers a balance of ease of use and advanced features, making it perfect for beginners.

Nikon D7500: A mid-range DSLR that offers a great combination of performance and portability, suitable for enthusiasts.

Pentax K-1 Mark II: A full-frame DSLR that is weather-resistant, making it ideal for outdoor photography.

Mirrorless Cameras

Digital Single-Lens Reflex (DSLR) cameras have long been a favorite among photographers due to their robust features, reliability, and the exceptional quality of images they produce. From beginners to seasoned professionals, DSLRs cater to a wide range of photography needs.

How they work:

The primary difference between mirrorless cameras and DSLRs is the absence of a mirror. Here's how they operate:

Direct Light Path: In a mirrorless camera, light passes directly through the lens and onto the image sensor without the need for a mirror to reflect it.

Electronic Viewfinder or LCD Screen: Instead of an optical viewfinder, mirrorless cameras use an electronic viewfinder (EVF) or the rear LCD screen to display the scene. This digital preview shows you how your final image will look, including any adjustments you make to settings like exposure or white balance.

Key Features:

Despite their smaller size, mirrorless cameras are packed with features that make them formidable contenders in the photography world:

Interchangeable Lenses:

Like DSLRs, mirrorless cameras allow for lens swapping, giving photographers the flexibility to choose the right lens for the job.

1

Compact Design:

The absence of a mirror makes these cameras lighter and more compact, making them ideal for travel, street photography, and situations where portability is key.

2

3

Real-Time Preview:
The electronic viewfinder allows photographers to see how changes in settings will affect the final image, which is particularly useful for beginners.

4

Advanced Video Capabilities:

Mirrorless cameras often excel in video recording, with many offering features like 4K resolution and high frame rates.

Advantages:

The versatility of DSLRs makes them suitable for almost any type of photography. Whether you're capturing portraits, landscapes, sports, or wildlife, a DSLR can handle the task. The availability of a wide range of lenses allows you to experiment with different focal lengths and perspectives. Additionally, the robust build quality of many DSLRs means they can withstand tough conditions, making them reliable tools for photographers in any environment.

Examples of Mirrorless Cameras:

Sony Alpha a7 III: A full-frame mirrorless camera known for its excellent image quality and fast autofocus.

Fujifilm X-T4: Offers a perfect blend of classic design with modern features, including 4K video recording and in-body stabilization.

Canon EOS R6: Impressive autofocus capabilities and 4K video recording, ideal for a range of photography and videography needs.

Nikon Z6 II: Known for its solid build quality and performance, it is a great choice for both professionals and enthusiasts.

Smartphones

In the last decade, smartphone cameras have become the most popular type of camera globally, revolutionizing the way we capture and share our lives. Their rise to prominence is driven by their sheer convenience—smartphones are always with you, ready to capture any moment in an instant. But beyond convenience, modern smartphone cameras have become incredibly sophisticated, boasting advanced technology that allows them to compete with dedicated cameras in certain situations.

How they work:

Smartphone cameras are designed with simplicity and ease of use in mind. Unlike DSLRs or mirrorless cameras, which feature interchangeable lenses, smartphone cameras typically come with fixed lenses. However, many modern smartphones are equipped with multiple lenses, each serving a different purpose:

1- **Wide-Angle Lens:** Captures a broader field of view, making it ideal for landscapes or group photos.

2- **Telephoto Lens:** Provides optical zoom capability, allowing you to get closer to the subject without losing image quality.

3- **Macro Lens:** Enables extreme close-up shots, perfect for capturing small details like textures or tiny objects.

While the hardware plays a crucial role, the real power of smartphone photography lies in the software. Advanced algorithms enhance image quality by processing data from the camera sensor, reducing noise, adjusting colors, and even simulating effects like shallow depth of field (bokeh). This software-driven approach allows smartphone cameras to achieve results that would typically require more complex and bulky camera equipment.

Key Features:

Smartphones are not only about capturing photos, they excel in convenience and connectivity, offering a seamless photography experience:

Portrait Mode:
Uses software to create a depth effect, blurring the background while keeping the subject in sharp focus, mimicking the look of professional DSLR photography.

1

Night Mode:
Allows for clearer, brighter photos in low-light conditions by taking multiple shots at different exposures and combining them into one image.

2

HDR (High Dynamic Range):

Automatically combines multiple exposures to create a photo with balanced highlights and shadows, ensuring that details are visible even in challenging lighting conditions.

3

Instant Sharing:

After capturing a photo, smartphones allow you to edit and share your images directly from the device. Social media integration means you can upload photos to platforms like Instagram, Facebook, or Twitter within seconds of taking them.

4

Editing Tools:

·Built-in editing apps provide a range of options to enhance your photos, from basic adjustments like brightness and contrast to more advanced features like filters and retouching.

5

Advantages:

The biggest advantage of smartphone photography is its accessibility. You don't need to lug around a heavy camera or worry about complex settings—just point, shoot, and share. This makes smartphones ideal for capturing spontaneous moments, documenting your daily life, or sharing experiences on social media. The convenience of having a powerful camera in your pocket means you're always ready to capture that perfect shot, whether it's a candid moment with friends, a beautiful sunset, or an unexpected event.

Moreover, smartphone cameras have democratized photography, making it accessible to everyone, regardless of their level of expertise. While they may not offer the same level of manual control or image quality as DSLRs or mirrorless cameras, the advancements in smartphone camera technology have closed the gap considerably. For most casual photographers, and even for some professional applications, a smartphone camera can deliver stunning results.

Examples of Smartphones Cameras:

Apple iPhone 14 Pro: Known for its exceptional image quality, advanced computational photography, and triple-lens system, including a telephoto lens for optical

Samsung Galaxy S23 Ultra: Features a high-resolution camera with advanced zoom capabilities and night mode, making it ideal for low-light photography.

Google Pixel 7 Pro: Praised for its computational photography prowess, especially in low-light conditions, and features like astrophotography mode.

Huawei P50 Pro: Offers a powerful camera system with multiple lenses, including a periscope telephoto lens for impressive zoom capabilities.

OnePlus 10 Pro: Known for its balanced camera system with natural color reproduction and a variety of shooting modes, including a specialized night mode.

Lenses: Your Creative Eye

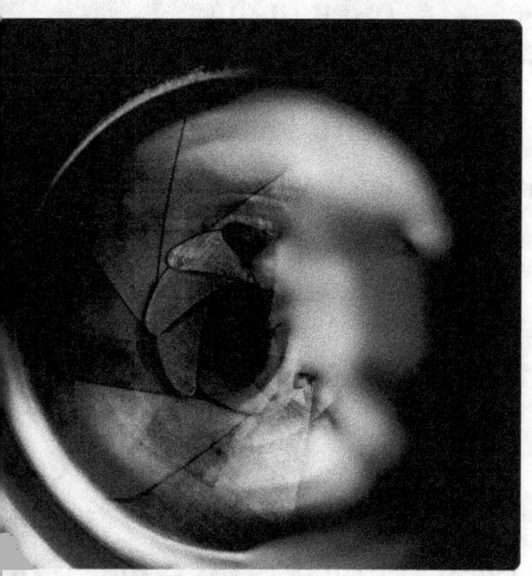

Lenses are one of the most important tools in a photographer's arsenal. The lens you choose determines the perspective, depth, and sharpness of your images. Here's an overview of different types of lenses and how they can shape your photography

a. Prime Lenses

Prime lenses have a fixed focal length, meaning they do not zoom. Common focal lengths include 35mm, 50mm, and 85mm. The advantages of prime lenses include:

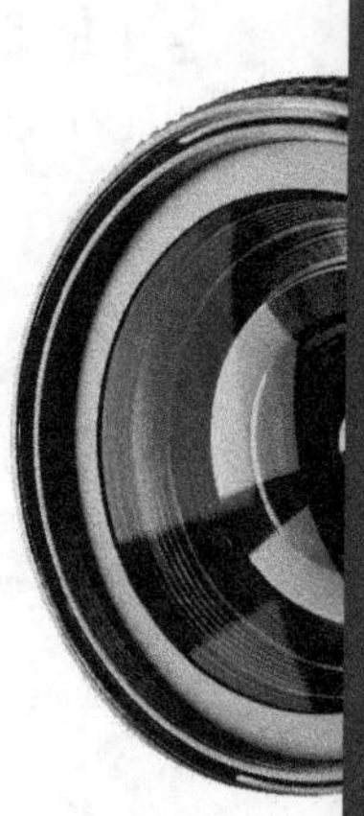

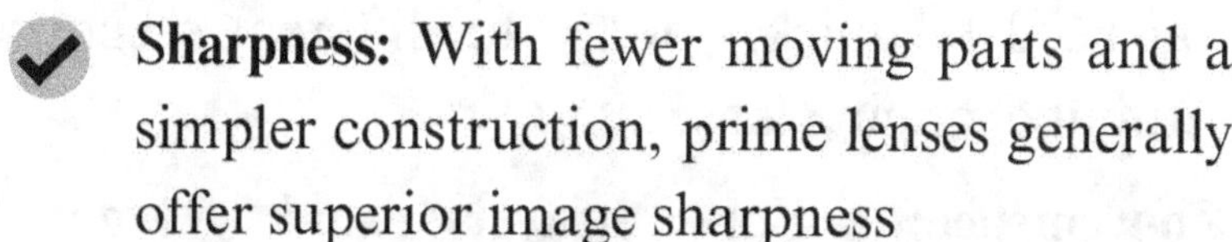

- **Sharpness:** With fewer moving parts and a simpler construction, prime lenses generally offer superior image sharpness

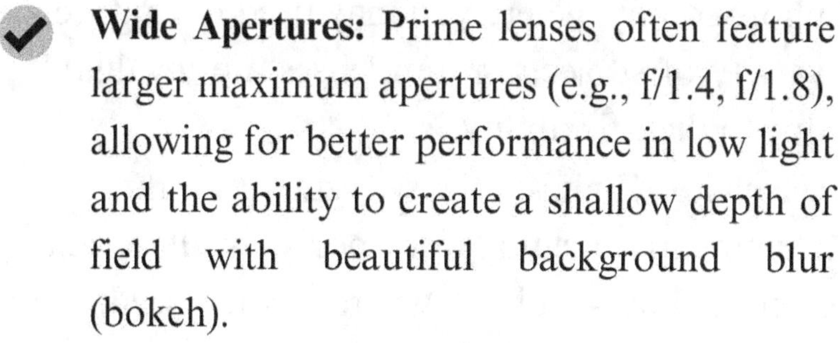

- **Wide Apertures:** Prime lenses often feature larger maximum apertures (e.g., f/1.4, f/1.8), allowing for better performance in low light and the ability to create a shallow depth of field with beautiful background blur (bokeh).

- ✅ **Lightweight:** Without the need for zoom mechanics, prime lenses are often lighter and more compact than zoom lenses.

Prime lenses are ideal for portraiture, street photography, and any scenario where you want to achieve the highest image quality with a distinct, creative look.

b. Zoom Lenses

Zoom lenses offer variable focal lengths, making them versatile tools for a wide range of photography styles. For instance, a 24-70mm zoom lens can cover wide-angle shots at 24mm and tighter compositions at 70mm.

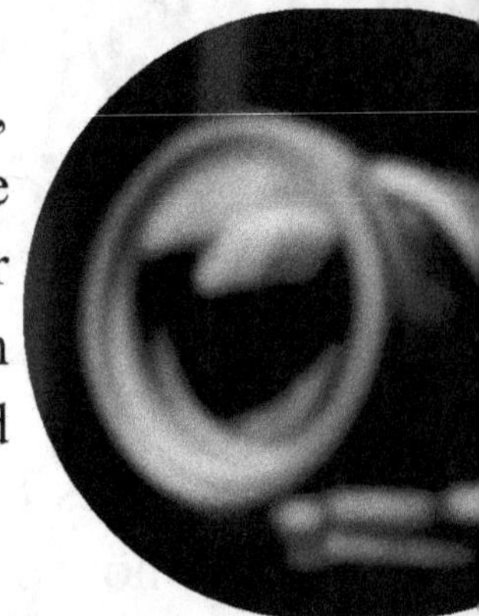

- ✅ **Versatility:** The ability to adjust the focal length makes zoom lenses perfect for situations where you need to quickly adapt to different scenes without changing lenses.

- ✅ **Convenience:** For travel and event photography, where you may need to capture a variety of subjects, zoom lenses are invaluable due to their flexibility.

- ✅ **Telephoto Zooms:** Lenses such as the 70-200mm are essential for sports, wildlife, and event photography, where you need to photograph subjects from a distance.

While zoom lenses are convenient, they may not offer the same level of sharpness and wide apertures as prime lenses, especially in the lower-end models. However, high-quality zoom lenses, often referred to as "professional zooms," can deliver outstanding performance.

c. Specialty Lenses

In addition to standard prime and zoom lenses, there are specialty lenses designed for specific purposes:

- **Macro Lenses:** These lenses are designed for extreme close-up photography, allowing you to capture minute details of small subjects like insects, flowers, or jewelry. Macro lenses typically have a 1:1 magnification ratio, meaning the subject appears life-sized on the sensor.

- **Wide-Angle Lenses:** With focal lengths typically ranging from 10mm to 35mm, wide-angle lenses are perfect for landscape, architectural, and interior photography. They capture a broader field of view, making them ideal for expansive scenes.

- **Telephoto Lenses:** These lenses have long focal lengths (e.g., 200mm to 600mm) and are used for capturing distant subjects. Telephoto lenses are essential for wildlife and sports photographers who need to bring distant action up close.

- **Fisheye Lenses:** These ultra-wide-angle lenses create a spherical, distorted image that is both creative and eye-catching. Fisheye lenses are often used for artistic, abstract photography.

Flash: Illuminating Your Subject

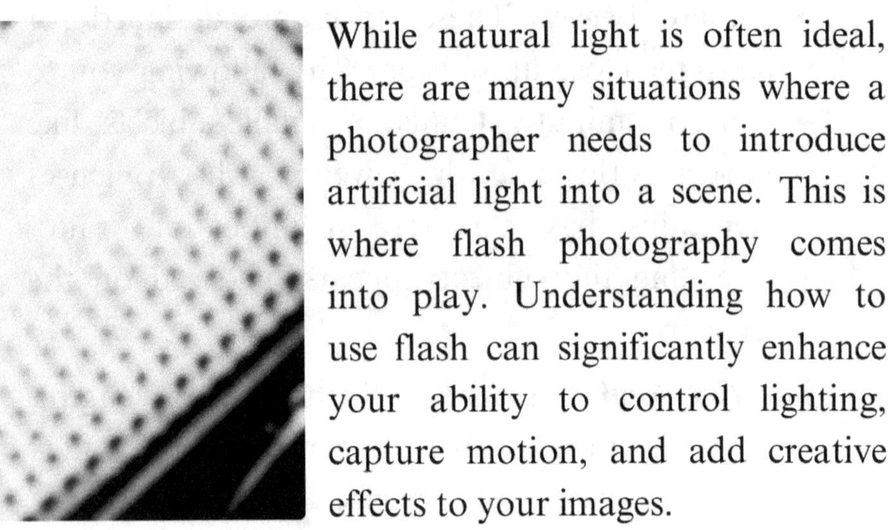

While natural light is often ideal, there are many situations where a photographer needs to introduce artificial light into a scene. This is where flash photography comes into play. Understanding how to use flash can significantly enhance your ability to control lighting, capture motion, and add creative effects to your images.

a. Built-in Flash

Most cameras come with a built-in flash. While convenient, the built-in flash is generally not very powerful and can produce harsh, direct light that leads to unflattering shadows and red-eye.

✔ **Uses:** Built-in flash is useful in emergencies or when you need a quick fill light to illuminate shadows in a backlit situation.

✔ **Limitations:** Due to its fixed position close to the camera lens, the built-in flash often results in flat, unflattering lighting.

b. External Flash (Speedlight)

An external flash, also known as a speedlight, is a versatile tool that attaches to your camera's hot shoe (or can be used off-camera) and provides more powerful and flexible lighting options.

✔ **Bounce Flash:** By angling the flash head to bounce light off walls or ceilings, you can soften the light and create a more natural look, mimicking ambient light.

✔ **Fill Flash:** In outdoor photography, especially in bright sunlight, an external flash can be used as fill light to reduce harsh shadows on your subject's face.

✔ **Off-Camera Flash:** By using wireless triggers, you can position the flash off-camera, giving you greater creative control over lighting direction and intensity. This is particularly useful for portrait photography.

c. Flash Modifiers

Modifiers are accessories that attach to your flash to shape and control the light. These include:

- **Diffusers:** These soften the light, reducing harsh shadows and creating a more even illumination.

- **Softboxes:** When used with a flash, softboxes create a large, soft light source that is perfect for portraiture and product photography.

- **Grids and Snoots:** These help focus the light into a narrower beam, allowing for dramatic lighting effects and greater control over where the light falls.

Basics of Camera Operation: Aperture, Shutter Speed, and ISO

Once you've selected your camera, the next step is mastering the core principles of camera operation to take full control of your photography. The foundation of this control lies in understanding three fundamental settings: aperture, shutter speed, and ISO. Together, these elements form what is known as the "exposure triangle," and they work in harmony to determine how much light reaches your camera's sensor. This, in turn, affects the exposure, how bright or dark your final image is. Mastering these settings is essential for moving beyond the automatic modes of your camera and truly expressing your creative vision.

Aperture

Aperture Size:

Aperture refers to the size of the opening in the lens that allows light to enter the camera. It is measured in f-stops (e.g., f/1.8, f/4, f/16), where the f-stop number represents the ratio of the lens's focal length to the diameter of the aperture. The lower the f-stop number, the larger the aperture opening, and the more light that enters the camera. Conversely, a higher f-stop number indicates a smaller aperture opening, allowing less light to pass through.

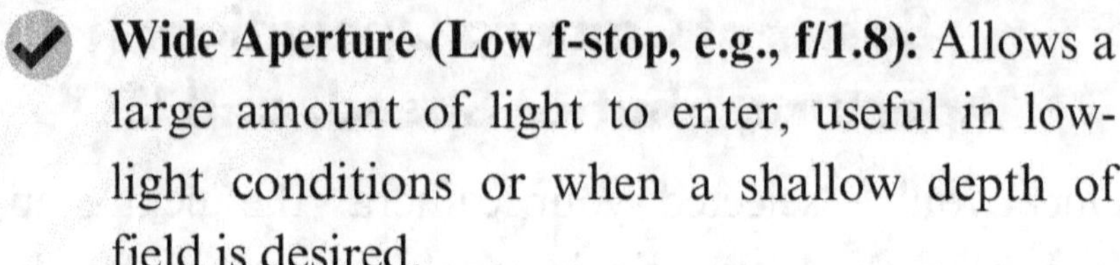

- **Wide Aperture (Low f-stop, e.g., f/1.8):** Allows a large amount of light to enter, useful in low-light conditions or when a shallow depth of field is desired.
- **Narrow Aperture (High f-stop, e.g., f/16):** Limits the amount of light entering the camera, which is helpful in bright conditions or when a greater depth of field is needed.

Effect on Depth of Field:

Depth of field refers to the range of distance within a photo that appears acceptably sharp. Aperture plays a crucial role in controlling depth of field:

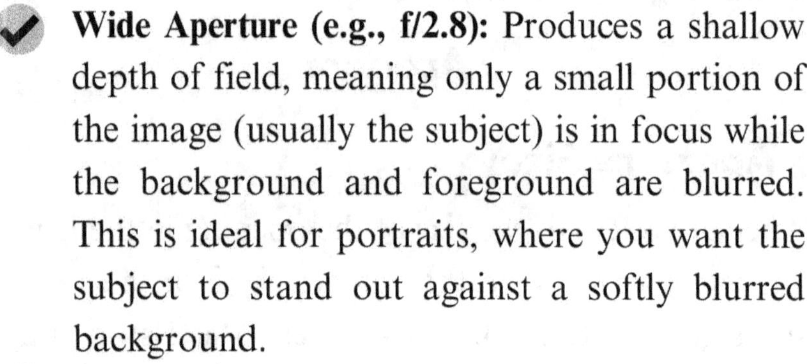

- **Wide Aperture (e.g., f/2.8):** Produces a shallow depth of field, meaning only a small portion of the image (usually the subject) is in focus while the background and foreground are blurred. This is ideal for portraits, where you want the subject to stand out against a softly blurred background.
- **Narrow Aperture (e.g., f/11):** Increases depth of field, making more of the scene in focus from the foreground to the background. This is beneficial for landscape photography, where you want both the foreground and distant elements to be sharp.

Effect on Exposure:

Aperture directly impacts the exposure of your image by controlling how much light reaches the sensor:

- **·Wide Aperture (e.g., f/2.0):** Allows more light to enter, making the image brighter, which is particularly useful in low-light situations.

- **Narrow Aperture (e.g., f/22):** Restricts the light entering the camera, resulting in a darker image, which can help avoid overexposure in bright conditions.

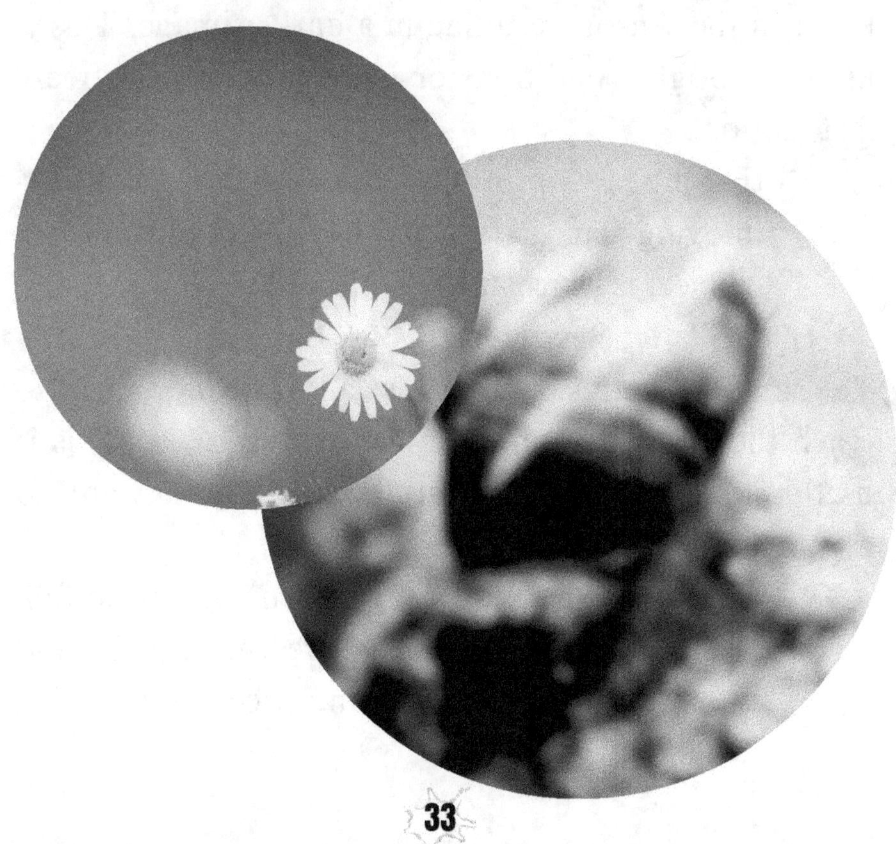

Shutter Speed

Shutter speed is the length of time the camera's shutter remains open, allowing light to hit the camera sensor. It is measured in seconds or fractions of a second (e.g., 1/1000s, 1/60s, 2s).

How It Works:

Shutter speed controls the duration of light exposure on the sensor. The longer the shutter is open, the more light is captured.

Effects on Exposure:

- **Fast Shutter Speed (e.g., 1/1000s):**

The shutter opens and closes quickly, allowing less light to reach the sensor, resulting in a darker image. This is useful in bright conditions or when you need to freeze fast motion.

  - Example: Capturing a bird in flight or a fast-moving car, a fast shutter speed ensures the subject is sharp and not blurred.

- **Slow Shutter Speed (e.g., 1/30s, 1s):**

The shutter remains open longer, allowing more light to reach the sensor, resulting in a brighter image. This is useful in low-light situations or when you want to capture motion blur.

  - Example: Shooting a night scene or a waterfall, a slow shutter speed captures more light and can create a smooth, flowing effect with moving water.

Effects on Motion:

- **Freeze Motion (Fast Shutter Speed):**
  - A fast shutter speed freezes motion, capturing sharp images of moving subjects. Ideal for sports, wildlife, or any action photography.
- **Motion Blur (Slow Shutter Speed):**
  - A slow shutter speed allows moving subjects to blur, conveying a sense of movement. This technique is used creatively in long exposure photography, such as light trails from cars or the smooth blur of water.

ISO

ISO measures the sensitivity of your camera's sensor to light. It is typically represented by numbers (e.g., ISO 100, ISO 400, ISO 1600).

How It Works:

A lower ISO number means less sensitivity to light and finer grain (noise) in the image, while a higher ISO number increases sensitivity but also increases noise.

Effects on Exposure:

- **Low ISO (e.g., ISO 100):**
  - Produces a clean, noise-free image with finer detail. This is ideal in bright conditions where there is plenty of light.
  - Example: Shooting in daylight or with studio lighting, a low ISO maintains high image quality.
- **High ISO (e.g., ISO 1600 or higher):**
  - Increases the camera's sensitivity to light, making the image brighter. However, it also introduces noise, which can reduce image quality.
  - Example: Shooting in low light, such as indoors or at night, a higher ISO allows you to capture brighter images without using a flash or slower shutter speed.

Effects on Image Quality:

- **Low ISO (Clean Image):**

At low ISO settings, the image quality is at its best with minimal noise. This is preferable for high-resolution images where detail is important.

- **High ISO (Increased Noise):**

As ISO increases, so does the amount of noise or grain in the image. While this is sometimes unavoidable in low-light situations, it's generally undesirable, especially in professional photography.

Balancing the Exposure Triangle

The key to mastering the Exposure Triangle is understanding how aperture, shutter speed, and ISO interact and balancing them to achieve the desired exposure and creative effect. Changing one element of the triangle affects the others, and finding the right balance depends on the shooting conditions and your creative intent.

Examples of Balancing the Exposure Triangle:

- **Scenario 1: Low-Light Indoor Portrait**
  - Wide Aperture (f/2.8): To allow more light in and create a soft background blur.
  - Slow Shutter Speed (1/60s): To ensure the image is bright enough without a high ISO, but still fast enough to avoid motion blur if the subject moves slightly.
  - Low ISO (ISO 400): To keep noise levels low while still brightening the image.

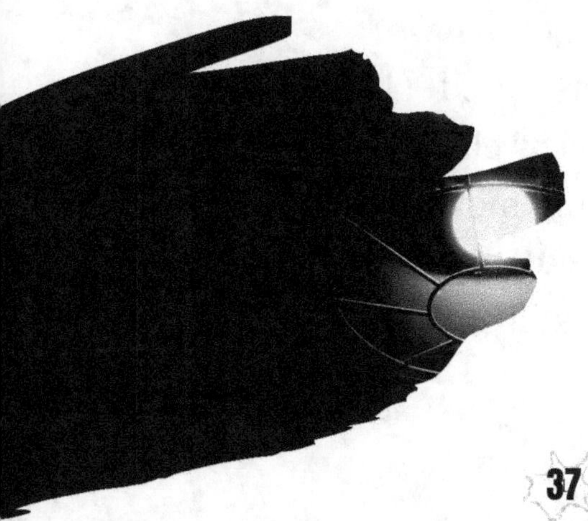

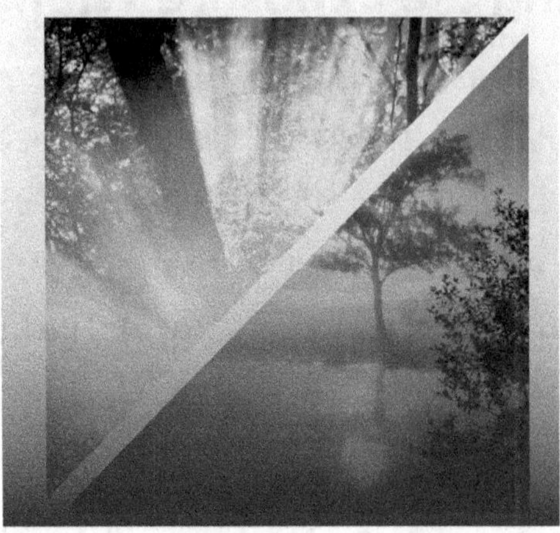

- **Scenario 2: Outdoor Landscape in Bright Sunlight**
  - Narrow Aperture (f/16): To achieve a deep depth of field, keeping the entire scene in focus.
  - Fast Shutter Speed (1/250s): To prevent overexposure in the bright sunlight.
  - Low ISO (ISO 100): To maintain maximum image quality with minimal noise.

- **Scenario 3: Nighttime Long Exposure**
  - Wide Aperture (f/4): To allow as much light as possible into the camera.
  - Very Slow Shutter Speed (10s): To capture enough light for a well-exposed image and create light trails from moving cars.
  - Low to Medium ISO (ISO 800): To avoid too much noise while still ensuring the image is bright enough.

Creative Control Through the Exposure Triangle

Understanding the Exposure Triangle not only helps in achieving correct exposure but also allows you to creatively control the outcome of your images. Here's how:

- **Aperture for Depth of Field Control:**
  Choose a wide aperture for portraits to blur the background and isolate the subject, or a narrow aperture for landscapes to keep everything in focus.

- **Shutter Speed for Motion Control:**
  Use a fast shutter speed to freeze action, or a slow shutter speed to convey motion through blur, as in long exposures or panning shots.

- **ISO for Light Sensitivity Control:**
  Adjust ISO to achieve the desired brightness while balancing noise levels, especially in challenging lighting condition.

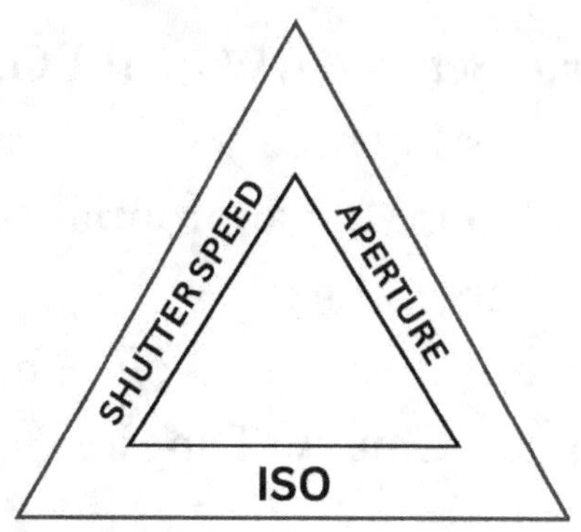

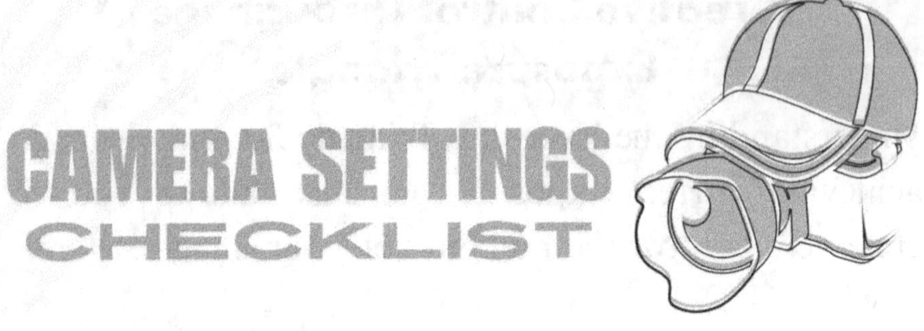

CAMERA SETTINGS
CHECKLIST

General Camera Preparation

- **Batteries Charged:** Ensure all camera batteries are fully charged.
- **Memory Cards:** Insert a memory card with ample space and format it if necessary.
- **Lens Clean:** Clean your lens with a microfiber cloth to remove any dust or smudges.
- **Camera Mode:** Set your camera to the appropriate mode (Manual, Aperture Priority, Shutter Priority, etc.).

Image Quality Settings

- **Image Format:** Set to RAW or JPEG, depending on your post-processing needs.
- **Image Size:** Choose the appropriate image size and quality (e.g., Large, Fine).
- **White Balance:** Adjust based on lighting conditions (Auto, Daylight, Cloudy, Tungsten, etc.).

CHAPTER THREE

Composition and Lighting

Photography is more than just pointing your camera and pressing the shutter button. It's about telling a story, evoking emotions, and highlighting subjects in a way that captures the viewer's attention. Two critical elements that can transform an ordinary photo into something extraordinary are composition and lighting.

Rule of Thirds and Leading Lines

Rule of Thirds

The Rule of Thirds is one of the most fundamental and widely used composition techniques in photography.

It's a simple guideline that can dramatically improve the balance and interest of your photos. Imagine your image is divided into nine equal parts by two horizontal and two vertical lines. The **R**ule of Thirds suggests that you should place the key elements of your scene along these lines or at their intersections. This create a more balanced and engaging composition. Instead of centering your subject, the Rule of Thirds encourages you to place it off-center, which adds dynamism and visual interest to the image.

Impact on Creating Balanced Compositions:

When you place your subject off-center according to the Rule of Thirds, you leave space for the environment, which can add context to your photograph. For example, in a landscape photo, placing the horizon along one of the horizontal lines instead of in the middle of the frame can make the image feel more expansive and balanced. In portraits, positioning the subject's eyes at one of the intersection points draws the viewer's attention to the most important part of the image, creating a more engaging photo.

Leading Lines

Leading lines are another powerful composition tool that can help guide the viewer's eye through your photograph and towards the main subject.

- **Using Lines in the Environment:** Leading lines can be found everywhere, in roads, rivers, fences, shadows, or even the natural curves of a landscape. These lines draw the viewer's eye through the image, leading them from one part of the scene to another, and ultimately to the main subject. The use of leading lines can add depth and dimension to your photos, making them more visually appealing.

- **Guiding the Viewer's Eye:** Strategically positioning leading lines in your composition will help you control how the viewer's eye moves through the image. For instance, a road leading into the distance can draw the viewer's gaze towards a mountain range, or a river can lead them towards a bridge. This technique is especially effective in architectural, street, and landscape photography, where the lines of buildings, paths, or natural features can be used to create a visual journey within the photo.

Lighting Basics
Understanding Natural and Artificial Light

Lighting is one of the most important aspects of photography. It affects not only the exposure of your image but also the mood, tone, and overall impact. Understanding how to work with both natural and artificial light is crucial for capturing the best possible photos.

Natural Light

Golden Hour: The Golden Hour is a magical time for photographers. It refers to the period shortly after sunrise and before sunset when the sun is low in the sky, casting a soft, warm, and diffused light. This lighting is perfect for creating romantic or serene atmospheres in your photos. The warm tones and long shadows add depth and richness, making your images more visually pleasing. Whether you're shooting landscapes, portraits, or anything in between, the Golden Hour is the ideal time to capture beautiful, natural light.

Blue Hour: The Blue Hour occurs just before sunrise and after sunset, when the sun is below the horizon, and the light is soft, cool, and blue in tone. This time of day is perfect for capturing moody, tranquil images. The soft blue light is ideal for landscapes, cityscapes, and any scene where you want to convey a calm, peaceful atmosphere. The Blue Hour can also be a great time for long exposure photography, capturing the movement of clouds or water in a serene and dreamy way.

Artificial Light

While natural light is wonderful, it's not always available or ideal. That's where artificial light comes in. Artificial light sources, such as lamps, flash units, or studio lights, can be controlled and manipulated to achieve the desired effect.

How Lighting Affects Mood and Tone: Light is a powerful tool that can set the mood and tone of your photograph. Harsh midday light can create dramatic shadows and high contrast, perfect for strong, intense images. On the other hand, soft evening light can evoke a sense of calm and nostalgia, ideal for portraits or romantic scenes. By understanding how different types of light affect your image, you can choose the right lighting to match the mood you want to convey.

Advanced Lighting Techniques
Rembrandt Lighting

Rembrandt lighting is named after the famous Dutch painter Rembrandt, who used this technique in many of his portraits. It's characterized by a small, triangular patch of light on the cheek of the subject's shadowed side. This effect is achieved by placing the main light source at a 45-degree angle to the subject and slightly above eye level.

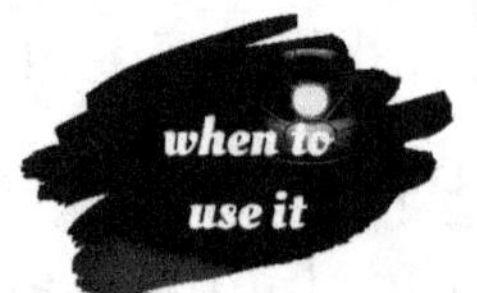

Rembrandt lighting adds depth and dimension to a portrait, making it look more dramatic and intense. It's especially effective for creating a moody or mysterious atmosphere. This technique is often used in portrait photography when you want to emphasize the structure of the face, highlighting the contours and creating a sense of depth.

Butterfly Lighting

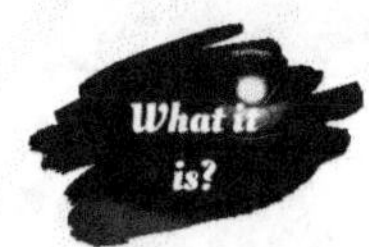

Butterfly lighting is named after the butterfly-shaped shadow that appears under the subject's nose when the light source is placed directly in front of and slightly above the subject. This technique is commonly used in beauty and glamour photography because it flatters the face by highlighting the cheekbones and creating a soft, even light across the skin.

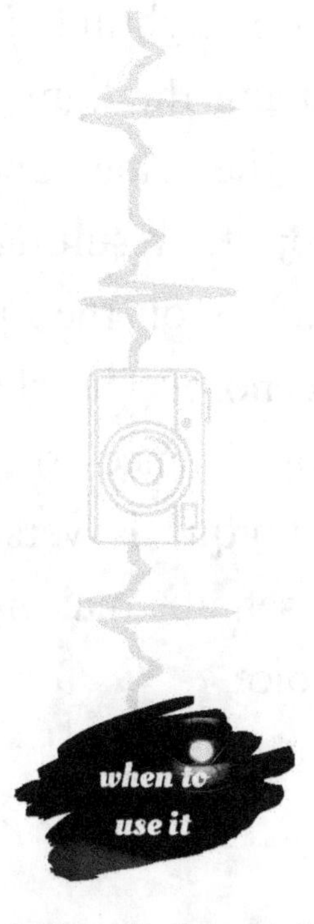

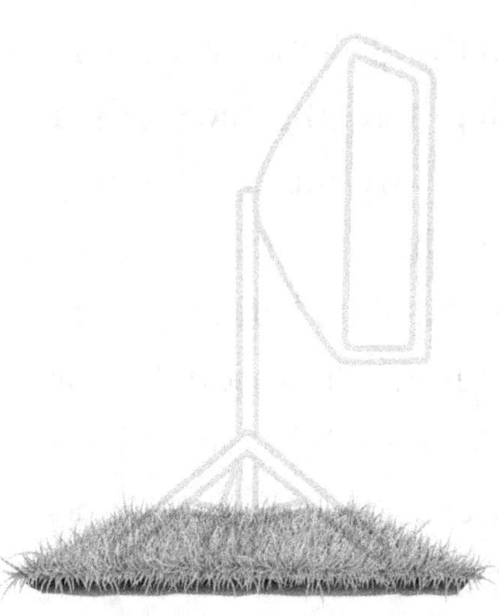

Butterfly lighting is ideal for creating a clean, glamorous look. It's flattering for most face shapes and is often used in fashion and beauty photography. This technique is also great for creating a more formal and polished portrait.

Loop Lighting

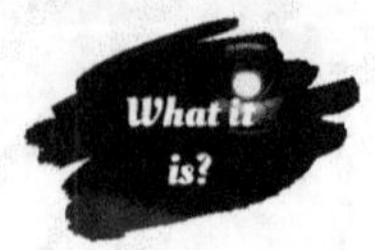

Loop lighting is created by placing the light source slightly to the side and above the subject, resulting in a small shadow on the opposite side of the nose. The shadow forms a loop, hence the name. This technique is versatile and easy to set up, making it a popular choice for portrait photographers.

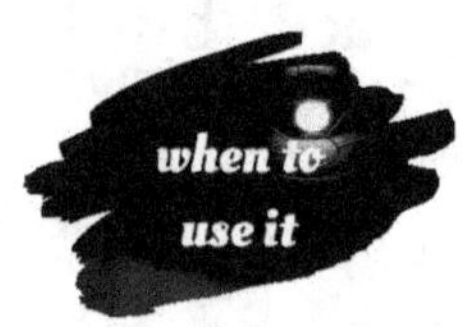

Loop lighting is ideal for creating a soft, natural look while still adding depth to the face. It's a great all-around lighting technique that works well for most portraits. Whether you're photographing individuals or groups, loop lighting can help you achieve a balanced and flattering image.

CHAPTER FOUR

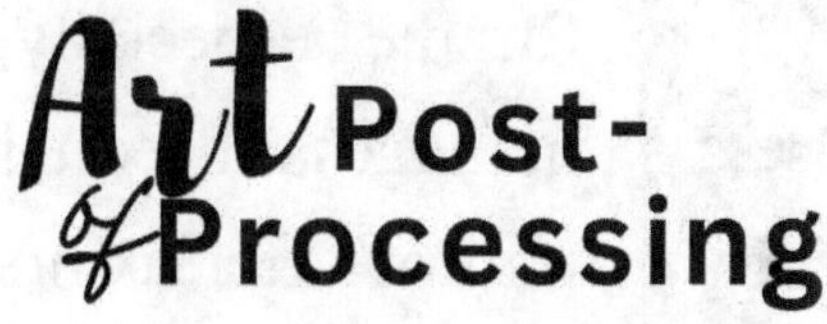

Post-processing is where photography truly becomes an art form. It's the stage where you can take a good photograph and turn it into something extraordinary. I remember when I first started exploring post-processing; it was like unlocking a whole new world of possibilities. The power to enhance, refine, and sometimes completely transform an image is both exhilarating and a little intimidating. But once you get the hang of it, post-processing becomes an essential part of your creative toolkit.

Introduction to Post-Processing Software

When I first started out, I was overwhelmed by the sheer number of editing software options available. However, I quickly realized that Adobe Lightroom and Photoshop were the industry standards for a reason. They each have their strengths, and learning to use them effectively has made a huge difference in my work.

Adobe Lightroom

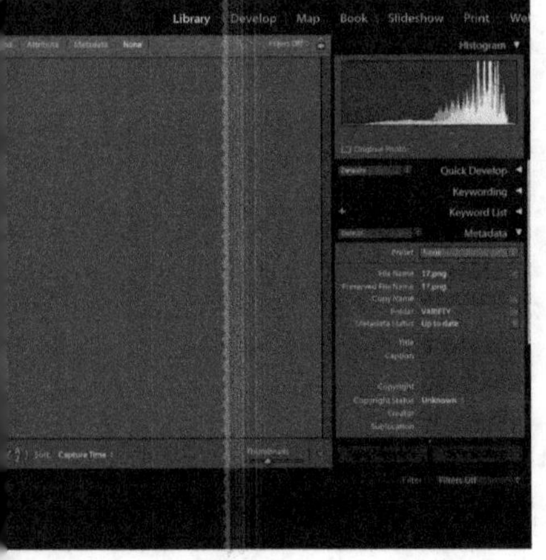

Lightroom was a game-changer for me, especially when I had to manage and edit large batches of photos after a shoot. Its ability to handle high volumes of images while still allowing for precise adjustments is something I rely on heavily.

Lightroom is like a digital darkroom designed specifically for photographers. What I love about it is the non-destructive editing process, it means I can experiment as much as I want without worrying about permanently altering my original images. The software saves all edits as separate layers, so you can always go back to your original photo if needed.

Key Features

✔ Develop Module

This is where I spend most of my time. The sliders are intuitive and responsive, making it easy to tweak exposure, contrast, and color balance. I remember being amazed at how a few simple adjustments could breathe new life into a photo.

✔ Presets

One of the best things about Lightroom is the ability to create and use presets. These are predefined settings that you can apply to multiple photos with a single click. Early on, I developed a few presets that matched my style, and they've saved me countless hours of editing time.

✔ Batch Processing

When I'm editing a large number of photos from a shoot, batch processing is a lifesaver. It allows me to apply the same adjustments to multiple images at once, ensuring a consistent look across the entire set.

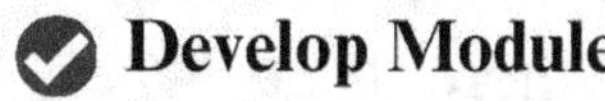

Adobe Photoshop

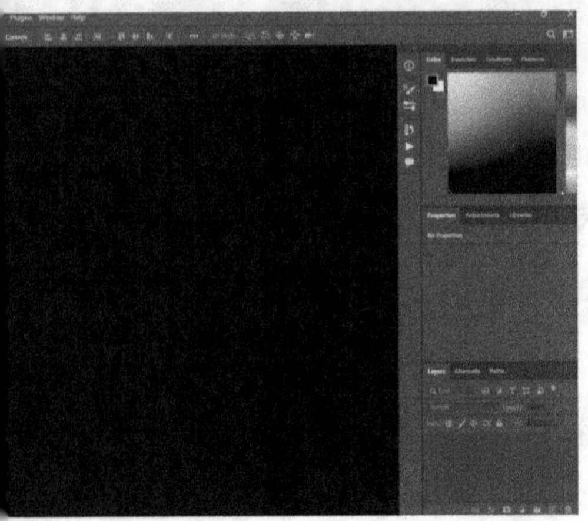

Photoshop, on the other hand, is where I go when I need to dive deep into an image. It's the tool I use for more detailed edits and creative manipulations, things that Lightroom just can't handle.

Photoshop is like having a complete artist's studio at your fingertips. It's where you can really get creative, whether you're retouching a portrait, creating a composite, or applying intricate effects. I'll admit, Photoshop can be a bit overwhelming at first, but once you learn the basics, the possibilities are endless.

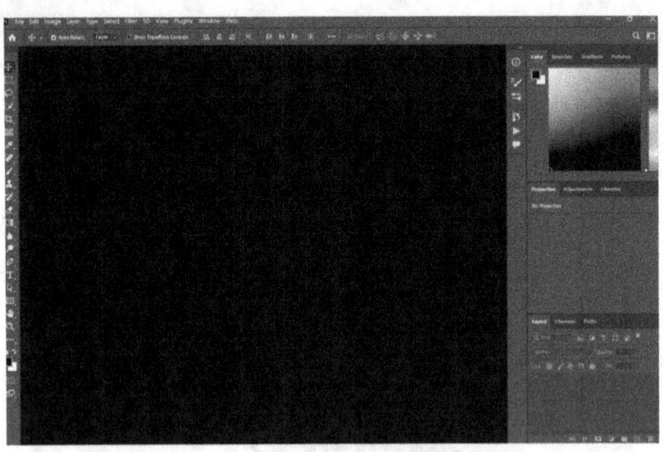

Key Features

✓ **Layers and Masks**

The layers system in Photoshop is incredibly powerful. It allows you to work on different aspects of your image separately, which is crucial for non-destructive editing. I often use masks to apply changes selectively, ensuring that I have complete control over every detail.

✓ **Selection Tools**

These tools are essential for making precise edits. Whether I'm isolating a subject, adjusting colors in a specific area, or removing unwanted objects, the selection tools give me the accuracy I need.

✓ **Creative Effects**

Photoshop's creative effects are where you can really let your imagination run wild. From adding textures to creating surreal compositions, the only limit is your creativity. I've spent countless hours experimenting with different effects, and it's one of the most rewarding parts of the process.

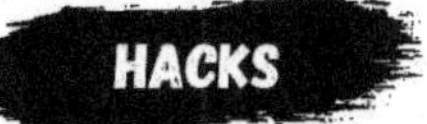

Basic Editing Techniques

Cropping

Cropping is probably one of the first editing techniques I learned, and it's one that I still use all the time. It's amazing how a simple crop can completely change the focus and feel of an image.

How to Crop Effectively

- **Aspect Ratios**

  I always pay attention to the aspect ratio when cropping. Whether I'm preparing an image for social media, printing, or a portfolio, maintaining a consistent aspect ratio helps keep my photos looking professional.

- **Removing Distractions**

  Cropping is my go-to method for eliminating distractions. If there's something in the background that takes away from the main subject, a quick crop can often solve the problem.

- **Enhancing Composition:**

  Sometimes, you don't get the composition perfect in-camera. Cropping allows you to adjust the framing according to the Rule of Thirds or other compositional guidelines, enhancing the overall balance and flow of the image.

Exposure Adjustments

Exposure is another key area where post-processing can save a photo. There have been plenty of times when I didn't quite get the exposure right in-camera, but Lightroom's exposure adjustments helped me recover the image.

How to Adjust Exposure

✅ **Exposure Slider**

The exposure slider is where I start when I need to brighten or darken an image. It's a simple adjustment, but it can have a big impact.

✅ **Highlights and Shadows**

I love using the highlights and shadows sliders to fine-tune the details. Bringing out details in the shadows or toning down overly bright areas can add depth and texture to an image.

✅ **Contrast**

Adding contrast can really make an image pop, but it's a delicate balance. Too much contrast, and you lose detail; too little, and the image looks flat. Finding the right balance is key.

Color Correction

Getting the colors just right is one of my favorite parts of the editing process. There's something incredibly satisfying about tweaking the white balance or adjusting the hues to create the exact mood I'm going for.

How to Correct Color

✅ **White Balance**

Adjusting the white balance is often the first step I take in color correction. Whether the image is too warm or too cool, getting the white balance right sets the foundation for the rest of the editing process.

✅ **HSL Adjustments**

I love playing with the HSL (Hue, Saturation, Luminance) sliders to fine-tune the colors. Whether I'm enhancing the blues in a sky or toning down the greens in a landscape, these adjustments help me achieve the perfect color palette.

✅ **Color Grading**

Color grading is where you can get really creative. I often use it to add a specific tone or mood to my images. Whether it's a warm, vintage feel or a cool, cinematic look, color grading helps me tell a story with my photos.

Advanced Editing

Retouching

Retouching is a skill that I've honed over time, especially when working with portraits. It's all about making the image look polished without losing its natural feel.

How to Retouch

- **Clone Stamp and Healing Brush**

  These tools are lifesavers when it comes to removing blemishes or unwanted elements. I use the Clone Stamp for larger areas and the Healing Brush for more precise work. It's all about subtlety, less is often more.

- **Spot Removal**

  This is my go-to tool for quickly getting rid of small imperfections. Whether it's a speck of dust on a product shot or a blemish on a portrait, the Spot Removal tool makes it easy.

- **Skin Smoothing**

  For portraits, skin smoothing can make a big difference. I use techniques like frequency separation to smooth skin while preserving texture, ensuring the result looks natural and not overdone.

Layer Adjustments

Layers are where Photoshop truly shines. Learning how to use layers effectively has been a game-changer for me, it's like having complete control over every aspect of the image.

How to Use Layers

- **Adjustment Layers**

  I use adjustment layers for everything from exposure and contrast adjustments to color corrections. Because they're non-destructive, I can tweak them as much as I want without affecting the original image.

- **Layer Masks**

  Masks allow me to apply edits selectively. For example, I might use a mask to brighten just the subject's face without altering the background. It's a powerful tool that gives me a lot of control.

- **Blending Modes**

  Blending modes are a fun way to experiment with how different layers interact. Sometimes, just changing the blending mode can create a whole new look or effect.

Creative Effects

This is where the real fun begins. Once you've got the technical aspects down, you can start exploring creative effects that push the boundaries of your photography.

How to Apply Creative Effects

✅ **Textures and Overlays**

I love adding textures or overlays to my images to create a unique look. Whether it's a subtle grain effect or a dramatic light leak, these additions can really enhance the mood of the photo.

✅ **Compositing**

Compositing is one of the most powerful tools in Photoshop. I've used it to combine multiple images into a single composition, creating everything from realistic scenes to surreal landscapes. It's a technique that takes practice, but the results can be truly stunning.

✅ **Artistic Filters**

Filters can be a quick and easy way to add a creative touch to your images. Whether you're going for a painterly effect or a high-contrast graphic look, filters allow you to experiment with different styles and techniques.

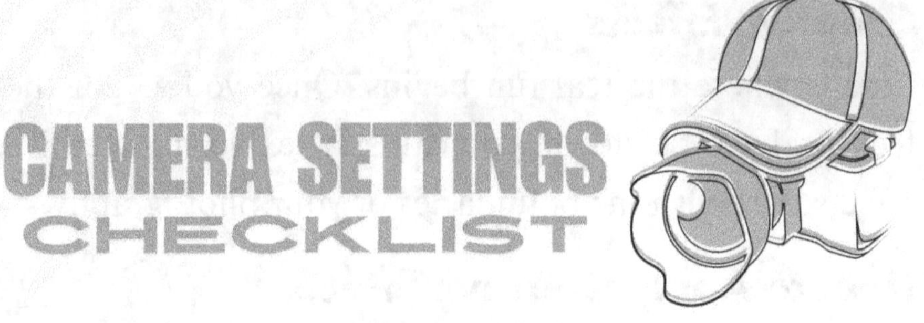

Exposure Settings

- **Aperture:** Set the f-stop according to the desired depth of field (e.g., f/2.8 for shallow depth of field, f/16 for deep depth of field).
- **Shutter Speed:** Adjust to capture motion or freeze action (e.g., 1/1000s for fast action, 1/30s for low light or motion blur).
- **ISO:** Set ISO based on lighting conditions (e.g., ISO 100 in bright light, ISO 800 or higher in low light).

Focus and Metering

- **Focus Mode:** Select the appropriate focus mode (Single, Continuous, Manual).
- **Focus Point:** Choose your focus point or set to automatic depending on the subject.
- **Metering Mode:** Set to Evaluative, Spot, or Center-weighted metering based on the scene.

CHAPTER FIVE

Types of Lighting in Photography

Natural Light

Natural light refers to light from the sun or moon, and it varies throughout the day and in different weather conditions. It is often preferred for its softness and natural feel but can be challenging to control.

As briefly highlighted earlier on, we will be talking deeply on the types of lighting and how to set up and combine different lighting to complement each other.

Settings and Use:

- Golden Hour: The hour after sunrise and before sunset, where the light is soft and warm. Ideal for portraits, landscapes, and anything needing a soft, flattering light.
- Midday Sun: The light is harsh and direct, casting strong shadows. Useful for creating dramatic effects, but can be difficult to manage for portraits.
- Overcast Day: The clouds diffuse the sunlight, creating a soft, even light that reduces shadows and highlights. Excellent for portraits and macro photography.
- Blue Hour: The time just before sunrise and after sunset, where the light is soft and blue-tinted. Ideal for creating moody, atmospheric images.

Artificial Light

Artificial lighting is any man-made light source, such as studio lights, LED panels, flash units, or household lamps. It offers full control over the lighting environment.

Types:

➤ Continuous Lighting:

Light that stays on constantly, allowing you to see how light and shadows fall on the subject in real-time. Examples include LED panels, fluorescent lights, and tungsten lights.

➤ Strobe Lighting: A flash of light that is typically more powerful than continuous lighting. Used in studio photography to freeze motion or illuminate a subject brightly.

➤ Speedlights

Compact, portable flash units that attach to the camera or can be used off-camera. Ideal for on-the-go shooting and filling in light in outdoor settings.

➤ Strobe Lighting: A flash of light that is typically more powerful than continuous lighting. Used in studio photography to freeze motion or illuminate a subject brightly.

Lighting Positions and Their Effects

1. Front Lighting

- **Position:** Light source is positioned directly in front of the subject, behind the camera.
- **Effects:**
  - Produces even, flat lighting with minimal shadows.
  - Highlights the entire subject, reducing the appearance of texture and depth.
  - Often used in product photography, passport photos, or when you want to minimize facial imperfections in portraits.
- **Output:** Front lighting creates a uniform and clear image but can be unflattering for portraits if not handled carefully, as it may make the subject appear flat and dimensionless.

2. Side Lighting

- **Position:** Light source is positioned to the side of the subject, at a 90-degree angle.
- **Effects:**
  - Creates strong shadows on the opposite side of the subject, adding depth and dimension.
  - Highlights texture and contours, making it ideal for showing the form and structure of an object or person.

- Commonly used in portrait photography for a more dramatic and artistic look, as well as in still life photography to emphasize texture.

- **Output:** Side lighting can produce dramatic contrasts, with one side of the subject illuminated and the other in shadow, creating a sense of depth and mystery.

3. Back Lighting

- **Position**: Light source is positioned behind the subject, facing towards the camera.

- **Effects:**
  - Creates a silhouette effect if the subject is not illuminated from the front.
  - Produces a rim light or halo effect around the subject, separating them from the background and adding a sense of depth.
  - Often used in outdoor photography during sunrise or sunset to capture silhouettes or in portraits to create a glowing outline around the subject's hair and edges.

- **Output:** Back lighting can either silhouette the subject or create a dreamy, ethereal effect by illuminating the subject's edges, making them stand out against the background.

4. Top Lighting

- Position: Light source is positioned directly above the subject.
- **Effects:**
    - Casts shadows directly downward, which can create deep shadows in the eye sockets, under the nose, and below the chin in portraits, giving a dramatic and sometimes sinister look.
    - Often used in product photography to highlight the top surfaces of objects or in architectural photography to simulate natural sunlight coming from above.
    - Used effectively in horror or noir-style photography for its intense shadow effects.
- **Output:** Top lighting creates strong shadows and highlights, emphasizing vertical structures and giving a powerful, often intimidating appearance.

5. Bottom Lighting

- Position: Light source is positioned directly below the subject, facing upward.
- Effects:
    - Reverses the natural direction of shadows, often creating an eerie or unnatural look.
    - Used primarily in horror photography and cinematography to create a spooky, unsettling effect.

- o In portrait photography, it's rarely used due to its unflattering nature but can be effective for dramatic or creative purposes.

- **Output:** Bottom lighting creates unnatural and dramatic effects, often associated with horror and suspense due to the unusual shadow patterns it creates.

Lighting Setups for Portraits

1. Rembrandt Lighting

- **Setup:** Light source is positioned at a 45-degree angle to the subject, and slightly above eye level. A small, triangular highlight appears under the eye on the shadow side of the face.

- **Effects:**
  - o Named after the painter Rembrandt, this lighting style adds depth and dimension to the face, with a distinct triangle of light on the cheek opposite the light source.
  - o Creates a balance between light and shadow, making it ideal for portraits that require a moody but still flattering look.

- **Output:** Rembrandt lighting produces a dramatic, painterly effect, highlighting facial features and adding a sense of mystery and depth.

2. Butterfly Lighting

- **Setup:** Light source is positioned directly in front of the subject and slightly above, creating a shadow under the nose that resembles a butterfly.
- **Effects:**
  - Flattering for most face shapes, as it highlights the cheekbones and produces a soft, even light across the face.
  - Often used in fashion and beauty photography to create a glamorous look.
- **Output:** Butterfly lighting creates a soft, flattering light that smooths skin textures and enhances facial contours, making it popular for beauty portraits.

3. Loop Lighting

- **Setup:** Light source is positioned to the side of the subject and slightly above eye level, creating a small loop-shaped shadow on the cheek opposite the light source.
- **Effects:**
  - Provides a balance between the soft, even light of butterfly lighting and the more dramatic shadows of Rembrandt lighting.
  - Ideal for creating depth while still maintaining a soft, flattering look for portraits.

- **Output:** Loop lighting adds gentle shadows and depth to the face, making it a versatile and flattering lighting style for most portrait situations.

4. Split Lighting

- **Setup:** Light source is positioned at a 90-degree angle to the subject, illuminating one half of the face while the other half remains in shadow.
- **Effects:**
  - Creates a very dramatic and bold effect, often used in male portraits or for creating a strong, mysterious vibe.
  - Highlights the texture and contours of the face, making it ideal for adding character and intensity to a portrait.
- **Output:** Split lighting produces a highly dramatic effect, dividing the face into a lit and a shadowed side, often used for intense or moody portraits.

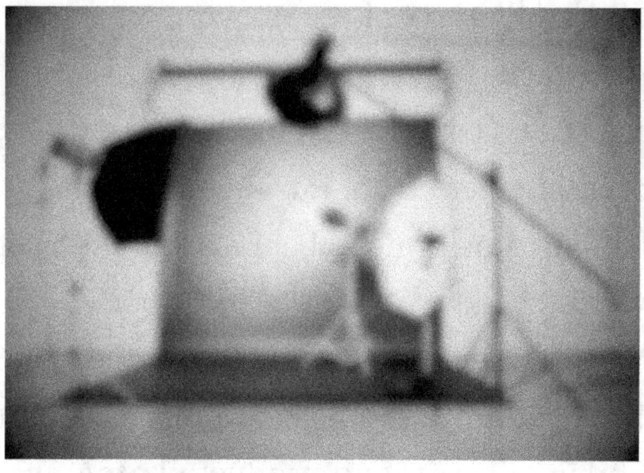

Using Multiple Light Sources

1. Key Light

- **Purpose:** The main light source, which determines the overall exposure and contrast of the image.
- **Position:** Typically positioned at a 45-degree angle to the subject and above eye level.
- **Effect:** The key light sets the mood of the photograph and is the primary light source around which all other lights are arranged.

2. Fill Light

- **Purpose:** To fill in shadows created by the key light, reducing contrast and softening the overall look.
- **Position:** Positioned on the opposite side of the key light, often at a lower intensity.
- **Effect:** The fill light balances the exposure, ensuring that shadows are not too dark and that details are visible in all areas of the image.

3. Rim (or Back) Light

- **Purpose:** To create a rim of light around the subject, separating them from the background.
- **Position:** Positioned behind the subject, aimed toward the back of their head or body.
- **Effect:** The rim light highlights the edges of the subject, adding depth and dimension, particularly useful in portraits and product photography.

4. Hair Light

- **Purpose:** Specifically to illuminate the hair, adding shine and separation from the background.
- **Position:** Positioned above and slightly behind the subject, aimed at the hair.
- **Effect:** The hair light adds a subtle glow to the hair, enhancing texture and preventing it from blending into dark backgrounds.

5. Background Light

- **Purpose:** To illuminate the background, adding depth and interest to the scene.
- **Position:** Positioned behind or to the side of the subject, aimed at the background.
- **Effect:** The background light separates the subject from the background and can create interesting patterns or gradients, enhancing the overall composition.

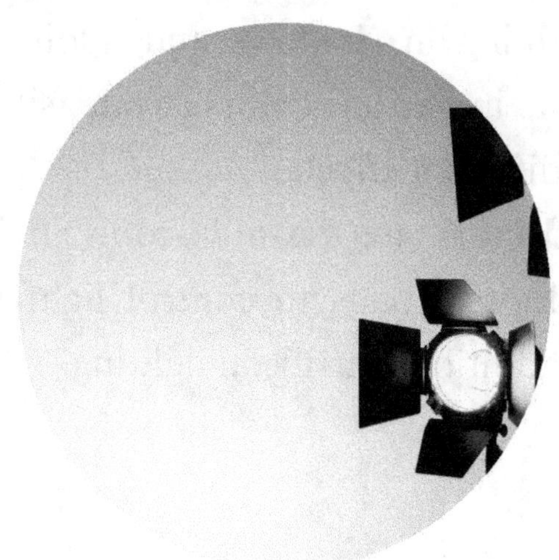

Light Modifiers and Their Functions

1. Softboxes

- **Function:** Softboxes diffuse light, creating a large, soft light source that reduces harsh shadows and provides even illumination.
- **Use:** Ideal for portraits, product photography, and any scenario where soft, flattering light is desired.

2. Umbrellas

- **Function:** Umbrellas spread light over a wide area, with shoot-through umbrellas producing soft, diffused light, and reflective umbrellas creating more focused, directional light.
- **Use:** Commonly used in portrait photography and as a cost-effective way to soften light.

3. Reflectors

- **Function:** Reflectors bounce light back onto the subject, filling in shadows and adding highlights. They come in various colors (white, silver, gold) to produce different effects.
- **Use:** Reflectors are versatile tools in both studio and outdoor settings to control light without the need for additional artificial lighting.

4. Grids

- **Function:** Grids narrow the beam of light, creating a focused, directional light with minimal spill. They are used to add contrast and control where the light falls.
- **Use:** Ideal for creating dramatic lighting effects, focusing light on specific areas of the subject, or adding texture and depth in portrait and product photography.

5. Gels

- **Function:** Gels are colored sheets placed over lights to change the color of the light. They are used for creative effects, balancing color temperature, or correcting color casts.
- **Use:** Common in theatrical photography, creative portraiture, and for adding mood or atmosphere by altering the color of the light.

Some Balanced and Effective Lighting Setup

1. Key Light (Softbox as the Main Light Source)

- **Positioning:**
  - The softbox is typically used as the key light, which is the main light source in your setup. Position the softbox at a 45-degree angle to the subject, slightly above eye level, and angled downwards. This positioning provides natural-looking, soft illumination, which is flattering for most subjects.

- **Direction:**
  - The light should be directed towards the subject's face or the area you want to highlight. The 45-degree angle helps to create shadows on one side of the face, adding depth and dimension while avoiding harsh shadows.

- **Complementing Lights:**
  - **Fill Light:** Place a fill light (another softbox, umbrella light, or reflector) on the opposite side of the subject, at a lower intensity, to fill in the shadows created by the key light. This balances the light, reducing contrast and softening shadows.

- **Rim Light:** Position a rim light behind the subject, aimed at the back of their head or shoulders, to create a rim of light that separates the subject from the background. A small softbox or a focused light source like a grid or snoot can be used here.
- **Hair Light:** If needed, place a hair light directly above or slightly behind the subject, aimed at their hair, to add shine and texture. This light should be subtle and focused.

2. Butterfly Lighting (Softbox Positioned Directly in Front)

- **Positioning:**
  - In a butterfly lighting setup, the softbox is positioned directly in front of the subject and slightly above, angled downwards towards the face. This setup creates a butterfly-shaped shadow under the nose, which is soft and flattering, especially for portraits.

- **Direction:**
  - The light is directed straight at the subject's face, which produces even lighting with minimal shadows. This positioning emphasizes the subject's facial features, particularly the cheekbones.

- **Complementing Lights:**
  - **Fill Light:** A reflector or a smaller softbox can be placed directly under the subject's face, angled upward, to fill in any shadows under the chin and eyes. This is often done with a white or silver reflector.
  - **Hair Light:** A hair light positioned above and slightly behind the subject adds separation from the background and highlights the hair. This can be a small softbox or a focused light with a diffuser.
  - **Background Light:** Position a light on the background to ensure it is properly illuminated, which helps in adding depth to the image.

3. Rembrandt Lighting (Softbox Positioned at 45 Degrees)

- **Positioning:** The softbox is positioned at a 45-degree angle to the subject, slightly above eye level, similar to the key light setup. However, in Rembrandt lighting, the softbox is placed further to the side, creating a triangle of light under the eye on the shadowed side of the face.
- **Direction:** The light is directed towards the subject's face, but with more emphasis on creating contrast between the lit and shadowed areas.

The goal is to achieve a natural but dramatic effect with distinct shadows.

- **Complementing Lights:**
  - **Fill Light:** Place a fill light at a lower intensity on the opposite side of the softbox, filling in some shadows without eliminating the characteristic Rembrandt triangle.
  - **Rim Light:** A rim light positioned behind the subject can add definition to the outline of the subject, enhancing separation from the background. Use a small softbox or a directional light source.
  - **Background Light:** Light the background to add depth, making sure it does not overpower the subject or cause unwanted reflections.

4. Loop Lighting (Softbox Positioned to the Side and Above)

- **Positioning:** The softbox is placed slightly to the side of the subject (around 30-45 degrees) and above their eye level. The goal is to create a small, soft shadow on the side of the nose, resembling a loop.

- **Direction:** Direct the light towards the subject's face at an angle that produces a loop-shaped shadow next to the nose, without creating harsh contrasts.

This lighting is flattering and versatile, making it ideal for most portrait situations.

- **Complementing Lights:**
  - **Fill Light:** Use a fill light on the opposite side, at a lower intensity, to soften shadows and provide a balanced exposure. This can be another softbox, an umbrella light, or a reflector.
  - **Hair Light:** Position a hair light above and slightly behind the subject to add a subtle highlight to the hair, enhancing texture and separation from the background.
  - **Rim Light:** If additional separation is needed, a rim light can be positioned behind the subject, slightly to the side, to add a soft edge light along the contours of the subject.

5. Split Lighting (Softbox Positioned at 90 Degrees)

- **Positioning:**
  - The softbox is positioned at a 90-degree angle to the subject, directly to the side. This setup creates a stark division of light and shadow, illuminating only one half of the face while the other half remains in shadow.

- **Direction:**
  - Direct the light straight across the subject's face to achieve a strong contrast between the lit and shadowed areas. This is a dramatic lighting setup that works well for creating intense, moody portraits.
- **Complementing Lights:**
  - **Fill Light:** You may use a very low-intensity fill light or reflector on the shadowed side if you want to soften the shadow slightly without losing the dramatic effect.
  - **Rim Light:** A rim light positioned behind the subject, on the same side as the key light, can help define the edges of the subject and separate them from the background.
  - **Hair Light:** If needed, add a hair light from above to illuminate the hair, ensuring it doesn't blend into the dark background.

6. **Three-Point Lighting Setup (Softbox with Complementary Lights)**
- **Key Light (Softbox):**
  - The softbox serves as the key light, positioned at a 45-degree angle and slightly above the subject. This light is the strongest and sets the tone for the overall exposure and shadow pattern.

- **Fill Light:**
  - A second softbox, reflector, or umbrella light is positioned on the opposite side of the key light to fill in shadows. The fill light is typically set at a lower intensity than the key light to maintain some contrast while reducing harsh shadows.
- **Rim/Back Light:**
  - A rim or backlight is placed behind the subject, aimed at their shoulders or the back of the head. This light helps to separate the subject from the background, adding depth and dimension.

CHAPTER SIX

Specialized Photography Setups

Every photography session has its unique set of challenges and opportunities, and understanding how to set up for different environments is key to capturing the best possible images. Over the years, I've found that preparation and the right setup can make all the difference between an average shot and an extraordinary one. It's time to talk about specialized photography setups for studios, indoor environments, and outdoor or event photography. These are the setups that I've come to rely on, and I'll share the insights I've gained from my experiences.

Studio Photography Setup

Studio photography offers the most control over all aspects of a shoot, lighting, background, and environment. I remember the first time I stepped into a professional studio; the possibilities seemed endless. The controlled environment allowed me to experiment and perfect my techniques without worrying about changing weather or lighting conditions.

Lighting Setup

Lighting is the cornerstone of studio photography. In the studio, you have the power to shape the light exactly how you want it, which is both liberating and a bit daunting when you're starting out.

Key Elements:

- **Softboxes and Umbrellas:** These are my go-to tools for diffusing light. Softboxes create a soft, even light that's perfect for portraits, while umbrellas can spread light over a larger area, making them ideal for group shots or product photography.
- **Strobe Lights:** Strobes are my favorite for freezing action and capturing crisp details. They're more powerful than continuous lights and allow you to control the intensity and duration of the light burst.
- Modifiers: I always have a few reflectors, grids, and diffusers on hand.

Reflectors help fill in shadows, grids focus the light to create more dramatic effects, and diffusers soften the light for a more flattering look.

Camera Setup

In the studio, precision is key. I typically use a tripod to ensure that the camera stays steady, especially during longer exposures. Tethering the camera to a computer is another trick I use; it allows me to see the images on a larger screen in real-time, making it easier to spot any issues.

Key Elements:

- **Tripod:** Essential for keeping the camera stable, especially when shooting with slower shutter speeds or when precise framing is needed.

- **Tethering:** Connecting the camera to a computer during the shoot lets me review images instantly. This helps in making quick adjustments and ensures I'm getting the shots I need.

- **Lens Choice:** I usually opt for a prime lens with a wide aperture (e.g., 50mm f/1.8) for portraits. The wide aperture allows for a shallow depth of field, which is great for isolating the subject from the background.

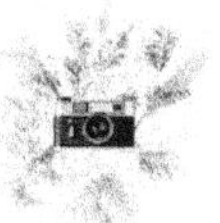

Background and Space Arrangement

The background is just as important as the subject. In the studio, I often use seamless paper or fabric backdrops in various colors, depending on the mood I want to create.

Key Elements:

- **Background:** Seamless paper backdrops are versatile and come in many colors. I also use fabric backdrops for more texture or when I want to create a specific ambiance.

- **Space Arrangement:** I always ensure there's enough space to move around the subject and adjust lights and equipment. Keeping the studio organized is crucial, there's nothing worse than tripping over cables during a shoot!

1

FINAL THOUGHTS ON STUDIO PHOTOGRAPHY

What I love most about studio photography is the control it offers. It's a space where I can fully experiment with light, composition, and subject interaction. Every session teaches me something new, and it's a constant process of refining techniques and trying out new ideas.

Indoor Photography Setup

Indoor photography can be both challenging and rewarding. Unlike in the studio, you're often working with existing light and space constraints, but that doesn't mean you can't create beautiful images. I've done shoots in everything from cozy living rooms to dimly lit cafes, and each setting brings its own set of considerations.

Lighting Setup

Lighting indoors often involves making the most of natural light or supplementing it with artificial sources. I've found that understanding how to manipulate available light is key to successful indoor photography.

Key Elements:

- **Natural Light:** Whenever possible, I use windows as natural light sources. The light they provide is soft and flattering, especially when diffused through curtains or sheer fabric.

- **Artificial Light:** When natural light isn't enough, I turn to lamps, portable LED panels, or even off-camera flash. Each light source can create a different mood, so I choose based on the feel I want for the photo.

White Balance: Indoor lighting can vary widely in color temperature, from the warm glow of tungsten bulbs to the cool tones of fluorescent lights. Adjusting the white balance on the camera helps ensure accurate color reproduction.

Camera Setup

Indoor environments often present challenges with low light, which can affect camera settings and the quality of the image. I typically use a faster lens and higher ISO settings to compensate.

Key Elements:

- **Handheld or Tripod:** Depending on the light, I might shoot handheld or use a tripod. A tripod is essential in low-light situations to avoid camera shake.
- **Lens Choice:** A lens with a wide aperture (like f/1.8 or f/2.8) is invaluable for indoor photography. It lets in more light, which is crucial when shooting in dim environments.
- **ISO and Noise Management:** Higher ISO settings help brighten the image in low light, but they can also introduce noise. I always balance ISO with aperture and shutter speed to minimize noise while still getting the right exposure.

Space Arrangement

Indoor spaces can be tight, so I always work with the environment to create the best composition. Sometimes that means rearranging furniture or shooting from unusual angles.

Key Elements:

- **Decluttering:** I start by clearing the area of any unnecessary items that could distract from the subject. Simplicity is key in creating a clean, focused image.

- **Using the Environment:** I look for interesting elements in the room that can add to the composition, like a patterned rug, a piece of art on the wall, or the way light falls on a surface.

2

FINAL THOUGHTS ON INDOOR PHOTOGRAPHY

Indoor photography is all about adapting to the space and making the most of the light available. It requires a bit of creativity and flexibility, but that's part of the fun. I've learned that with the right approach, even the most ordinary indoor settings can yield extraordinary photos.

Outdoor and Event Photography Setup

Outdoor and event photography is where things get really exciting. The unpredictability of natural light, the spontaneity of events, and the variety of settings make this type of photography both challenging and incredibly rewarding. I've shot everything from serene landscapes to high-energy concerts, and each experience has taught me the importance of preparation and adaptability.

Outdoor Photography Setup

When shooting outdoors, you're at the mercy of the elements, but with the right setup, you can capture stunning images regardless of the conditions.

Lighting Setup

Natural light is your primary source outdoors, and understanding how to work with it is crucial. I always pay attention to the time of day and the quality of light.

Key Elements:

- **Golden Hour:** The hour after sunrise and before sunset is my favorite time to shoot. The light is soft, warm, and flattering, making it perfect for everything from landscapes to portraits.
- **Midday Sun:** Shooting at midday can be challenging due to harsh shadows, but it's not impossible.

- Weather Considerations: I always check the weather forecast before heading out. Overcast days can provide beautiful, diffused light, while clear skies might call for filters to manage the brightness.

Camera Setup

In the great outdoors, flexibility is key. I need to be ready to adjust my settings on the fly as the light and conditions change.

Key Elements:

- **Portable Setup:** A lightweight tripod and a good camera strap are essential for mobility. I often find myself hiking to get the perfect shot, so keeping my gear light and accessible is a priority.
- **Lens Choice:** I typically carry a wide-angle lens for landscapes, a telephoto for distant subjects, and a prime lens for close-ups or portraits. This versatility allows me to capture a wide range of scenes.
- **Weather Protection:** I always have rain covers or plastic bags to protect my gear in case of sudden weather changes. You never know when a perfect shot might require standing in the rain!

Event Photography Setup

Event photography is all about capturing the energy and emotion of the moment. Whether it's a wedding, a concert, or a corporate event, the key is to be prepared for anything.

Lighting Setup

Events often have unpredictable lighting, so being able to adapt quickly is essential.

Key Elements:

- **Ambient Light:** I try to make the most of the existing lighting at the venue. Whether it's stage lights at a concert or the soft glow of candles at a wedding, ambient light can add atmosphere to the photos.
- **Flash:** Off-camera flash or speedlights are often necessary, especially in low-light venues. I prefer to bounce the flash off walls or ceilings to create softer, more natural light.
- **Continuous Lighting:** For events where video is also being shot, continuous lighting can provide consistent illumination. I use portable LED panels that are easy to set up and adjust.

Camera Setup

Events are fast-paced, so my camera setup needs to be ready to capture fleeting moments.

Key Elements:

- Multiple Cameras: If possible, I use two cameras with different lenses. This allows me to switch quickly between wide-angle shots and close-ups without missing a beat.

- **Backup Equipment:** I always bring extra batteries, memory cards, and even a second camera body. The last thing you want at an event is to run out of power or storage!

3

FINAL THOUGHTS ON OUTDOOR AND EVENT PHOTOGRAPHY

Outdoor and event photography are about being prepared, staying flexible, and thinking on your feet. It's a dynamic environment where the unexpected often leads to the most memorable shots. The more I shoot in these settings, the more I appreciate the challenges and the incredible opportunities they present.

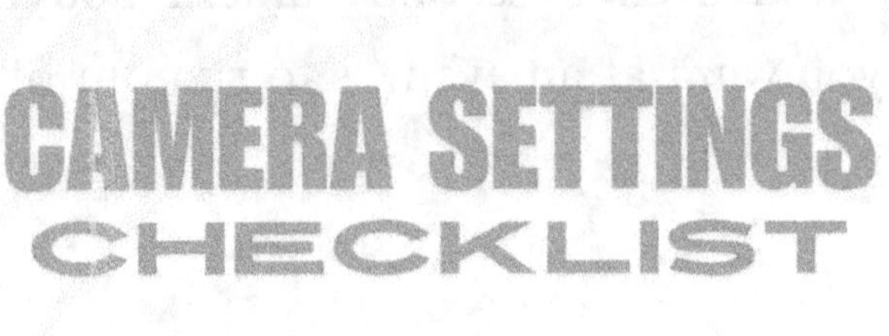
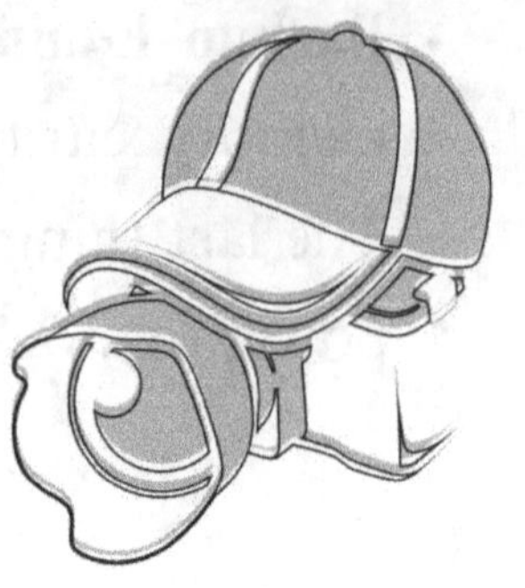

CAMERA SETTINGS
CHECKLIST

Shooting Mode Settings

- **Drive Mode:** Choose Single Shot, Continuous, or Timer, depending on your needs.
- **Exposure Compensation:** Adjust if necessary to lighten or darken the image.
- **Flash Settings:** Check if the flash is needed; adjust the flash power or use an external flash if required.

Specialized Settings

- **Stabilization:** Turn on/off Image Stabilization (IS) or Vibration Reduction (VR) depending on whether you're using a tripod.
- **Bracketing:** Set up exposure bracketing if shooting HDR.
- **Long Exposure Noise Reduction:** Turn on if shooting long exposures.

CHAPTER SEVEN

Practical Tips for Aspiring Photographers

As someone who has navigated the journey from beginner to professional photographer, I know firsthand the importance of practical advice. These tips aren't just theory, they come from real-world experience, trial and error, and learning what truly works in the field. Whether you're just starting out or looking to refine your skills, this chapter will guide you through the essential aspects of photography, from conceptualization to capturing the perfect shot, and finally, sharing your work with the world.

NOTABLES

1. Conceptualization and Planning

- Inspiration:
  - Every photograph begins with an idea or inspiration. This could come from a specific scene, a story you want to tell, or an emotion you wish to convey.
- Pre-Visualization:
  - Imagine the final image in your mind. Consider the mood, composition, and lighting that will best capture the moment you're envisioning.
- Research and Location Scouting:
  - For certain types of photography (e.g., landscapes, street photography), scouting locations in advance can be crucial. Consider the time of day, weather conditions, and the setting you want to use.
- Equipment Preparation:
  - Ensure your camera gear is ready. This includes charging batteries, formatting memory cards, selecting the appropriate lenses, and packing any additional equipment like tripods, filters, or lighting.

2. Capturing the Image

- **Setting Up:**
  - Once on location, take time to set up your camera and compose your shot. This involves choosing the right angle, framing your subject, and deciding on the focal length.
- **Technical Settings:**
  - Adjust your camera settings based on the conditions and the effect you want to achieve:
    - Aperture: Control depth of field.
    - Shutter Speed: Capture motion or freeze action.
    - ISO: Adjust sensitivity to light while balancing noise.
    - White Balance: Ensure accurate color representation.
- **Composition:**
  - Apply compositional techniques such as the Rule of Thirds, leading lines, symmetry, or framing to create a balanced and visually appealing image.
- **Lighting:**
  - Evaluate the lighting conditions. Decide whether natural light suffices or if you need to use artificial lighting or reflectors. Adjust the exposure to match the desired mood.

- **Taking the Shot:**
  - Capture multiple shots with varying settings if necessary. This increases your chances of getting the perfect shot, especially in dynamic or fast-changing environments.
- **Reviewing the Image:**
  - Quickly review your shots on the camera's display to check for focus, exposure, and composition. Make adjustments and retake shots if necessary.

3. Post-Capture Review

- **Uploading and Backing Up:**
  - Transfer your images to a computer and back them up. Organize your files by date, project, or subject for easy retrieval later.
- **Initial Selection:**
  - Go through your images and select the best ones for editing. Consider sharpness, composition, and emotional impact when making your choices.

4. Post-Processing

- **Basic Edits:**
  - Begin with global adjustments in software like Adobe Lightroom:
    - Cropping: Improve composition by removing distractions or adjusting the aspect ratio.
    - Exposure: Fine-tune the brightness and contrast.
    - White Balance: Correct any color casts for accurate color representation.
    - Color Correction: Adjust vibrancy and saturation to enhance the overall look.

- **Advanced Edits:**
  - Move into Adobe Photoshop for more detailed work:
    - Retouching: Remove blemishes, unwanted objects, or distractions.
    - Layer Adjustments: Use layers for non-destructive editing, including dodging and burning, adding textures, or applying special effects.
    - Creative Effects: Experiment with filters, textures, or composites to achieve a unique artistic vision.

- **Final Review:**
  - Compare the edited image with the original to ensure the adjustments enhance the photo without losing its original intent. Make any final tweaks as necessary.

5. Exporting and Sharing

- **Exporting:**
  - **Save your final images in the appropriate formats for different uses (e.g., JPEG for web, TIFF for printing).**
  - **Consider the resolution and file size based on how you plan to share or display the image.**
- **Sharing:**
  - Publish your work on social media, photography platforms, or your portfolio. If printing, ensure the colors and quality are up to standard.
  - Consider writing a brief caption or story to accompany your image, providing context or insights into the moment captured.
- **Archiving:**
  - Organize and archive your final images, ensuring they are backed up securely for future reference or use.

Glossary

Aperture:

The opening in a camera lens that controls the amount of light entering the camera. Aperture size is measured in f-stops (e.g., f/2.8, f/11), with lower numbers indicating a larger aperture that lets in more light and creates a shallow depth of field.

Aspect Ratio:

The proportional relationship between the width and height of an image, typically expressed as width (e.g., 3:2, 16:9). It determines the shape of the photograph.

Bokeh:

The aesthetic quality of the blur produced in the out-of-focus parts of an image, particularly in the background. Bokeh is often achieved by using a wide aperture and is prized for its soft, pleasing effect.

Bracketing:

A technique in which multiple photos are taken of the same scene at different exposures, allowing photographers to choose the best exposure or combine them into an HDR image.

Burst Mode (Continuous Shooting):

A camera setting that allows multiple photographs to be taken in quick succession by holding down the shutter button. It's useful for capturing fast-moving subjects.

Camera Obscura:

An early optical device that projects an image of its surroundings onto a screen. It's the precursor to the modern camera.

Chromatic Aberration:

A type of distortion where colors are incorrectly rendered at the edges of objects, often seen as a fringe of color along boundaries that separate dark and bright parts of the image.

Composition:

The arrangement of elements within a photograph. Key techniques include the Rule of Thirds, leading lines, symmetry, and framing.

Depth of Field (DoF):

The range of distance within a photo that appears sharp. A shallow depth of field means only a small part of the image is in focus, while a deep depth of field means most of the image is in focus.

Digital Single-Lens Reflex (DSLR):

A type of digital camera that uses a mirror mechanism to reflect light from the lens up into an optical viewfinder, allowing the photographer to see exactly what the lens sees.

Dynamic Range:

The range of light intensity from the darkest shadows to the brightest highlights in a photograph. A higher dynamic range means more detail in both the shadows and highlights.

Exposure:

The amount of light that reaches the camera's sensor, determined by the combination of aperture, shutter speed, and ISO. Correct exposure results in an image that is neither too dark nor too bright.

Exposure Compensation:

A camera setting that allows you to manually adjust the exposure level, making the image brighter or darker than what the camera's meter suggests.

Exposure Triangle:

A model that describes the relationship between aperture, shutter speed, and ISO. These three elements work together to control the exposure of an image.

F-Stop:

A unit of measurement that defines the aperture size. Lower f-stop numbers (e.g., f/2.8) mean a larger aperture and more light entering the camera, while higher f-stop numbers (e.g., f/16) mean a smaller aperture and less light.

Fill Light:

A secondary light source used to fill in shadows and reduce contrast in a scene, usually placed opposite the key light.

Flash:

A device that produces a burst of light to illuminate a scene. Flashes can be built into the camera or external.

Focal Length:

The distance between the lens and the image sensor when the subject is in focus, usually measured in millimeters (mm). Focal length affects the field of view and magnification of the image.

Golden Hour:

The period shortly after sunrise and before sunset when the light is soft, warm, and diffused. It's ideal for photography due to its flattering and rich tones.

HDR (High Dynamic Range):

A technique that combines multiple exposures of the same scene to create a single image with a greater dynamic range of lighting, capturing more detail in both the shadows and highlights.

Histogram:

A graphical representation of the tonal values in an image, showing the distribution of pixels from black (left) to white (right). It helps in assessing exposure.

ISO:

A measure of the camera sensor's sensitivity to light. Lower ISO values (e.g., ISO 100) produce cleaner images with less noise, while higher ISO values (e.g., ISO 1600) increase sensitivity but also introduce more noise.

JPEG:

A commonly used format for digital images, especially for those intended for web use. JPEGs compress image data, which reduces file size but can also reduce image quality.

Key Light:

The main light source in a photography setup, which determines the overall lighting and mood of the scene.

Leading Lines:

Lines within a photo that lead the viewer's eye to the main subject or through the composition. They can be roads, rivers, fences, or even shadows.

Lens:

The optical component of a camera that focuses light onto the sensor. Lenses come in various types, including prime (fixed focal length), zoom (variable focal length), wide-angle, telephoto, and macro.

Long Exposure:

A photographic technique that involves using a slow shutter speed to capture stationary elements while blurring moving elements, creating a sense of motion in the image.

Manual Mode (M):

A camera setting where the photographer has full control over all exposure settings, including aperture, shutter speed, and ISO.

Metering:

The process by which the camera measures the brightness of a scene to determine the correct exposure. Different metering modes include Evaluative, Spot, and Center-weighted.

Mirrorless Camera:

A type of digital camera that lacks the mirror mechanism found in DSLRs, resulting in a more compact design. Light passes directly from the lens to the image sensor, and the image is displayed on an electronic viewfinder or screen.

Noise:

The digital equivalent of grain in film photography, appearing as random specks or colored pixels in an image, particularly in low-light conditions or at high ISO settings.

Overexposure:

A condition where too much light reaches the camera's sensor, resulting in an image that is too bright, with loss of detail in the highlights.

Panning:

A technique used to capture motion by moving the camera in the same direction as a moving subject during exposure, resulting in a sharp subject with a blurred background.

Pixel:

The smallest unit of a digital image, each pixel represents a single point of color or brightness in the overall picture.

Post-Processing:

The process of editing and enhancing images using software like Adobe Lightroom or Photoshop after they have been captured. This can include adjusting exposure, color correction, cropping, retouching, and applying creative effects.

Prime Lens:

A lens with a fixed focal length (e.g., 50mm), known for its sharpness and wide maximum aperture.

RAW:

A file format that captures all the data from the camera's sensor without compression. RAW files offer greater flexibility in post-processing but require more storage space than JPEGs.

Rule of Thirds:

A compositional guideline that suggests dividing the image into nine equal parts by two equally spaced horizontal lines and two equally spaced vertical lines, placing the main subject along these lines or at their intersections.

Shutter Speed:

The length of time the camera's shutter remains open to allow light to reach the sensor. It's measured in seconds or fractions of a second (e.g., 1/1000s, 1s). Shutter speed affects exposure and motion blur.

Stabilization:

A feature in cameras and lenses that reduces the impact of camera shake, allowing for sharper images at slower shutter speeds.

Telephoto Lens:

A type of lens with a long focal length that brings distant subjects closer, often used for wildlife, sports, and portrait photography.

Underexposure:

A condition where too little light reaches the camera's sensor, resulting in an image that is too dark, with loss of detail in the shadows.

Viewfinder:

The part of the camera you look through to compose and focus your shot. On DSLRs, this is an optical viewfinder, while on mirrorless cameras, it's often an electronic display.

White Balance:

A camera setting that adjusts the color temperature of the image to ensure that whites appear white, and other colors are accurately represented under different lighting conditions (e.g., daylight, tungsten, fluorescent).

Wide-Angle Lens:

A lens with a short focal length that captures a wide field of view, often used in landscape, architectural, and interior photography.

Zoom Lens:

A lens with a variable focal length, allowing the photographer to zoom in and out on a subject without changing lenses.

www.ingramcontent.com/pod-product-compliance
Lightning Source LLC
Chambersburg PA
CBHW072102150726
47999CB00005B/1841